AF879673

The Separated Parents Handover Book

- Communication Book

by Daniel Francis

& D. Francis

ISBN: 978-0-9928548-9-8 (DF Books Limited)

DF Books Limited
www.13june2005.com

Cover Picture via Adobe - Royalty Free.
Interior Images Licensed from a Royalty Free Source.

This book is produced for educational purposes.

To the extent that third party sources have been used, fair use is sought.
This book has been produced for educational purposes.

Disclaimer: The authors and the publisher are not engaged in providing professional services. For the avoidance of doubt, if legal advice , child law advice, relationship advice or other professional services are required, such professional advice should be obtained from a suitably qualified practitioner. This work (or any promotional materials) is not legal advice, child law advice, relationship advice, or professional services and no reliance should be placed on it. All and any claims that this work (or any promotional materials) provides professional advice of any kind shall be denied and defended. The authors and the publisher are not responsible for the entries made or omitted in this book, or for the loss of data if the book is lost, misplaced, stolen or any other incident or occurrence. The authors and the publisher are not responsible for the entries made, or the consequences that might result thereafter. The authors and the publisher disclaim any and all liability in this jurisdiction or elsewhere, however it may be caused and shall not be responsible for any damages, financial loss, other detriment or costs. No warranty is provided.

Grandfa
Grandma
FAMILY
lovely
MOMMY
FRIENDS
Sweet
uncle
PARENTS
I my
family
AUNT
Grand
parents
MOTHER
DADDY
son
SISTER
Home
FATHER
BROTHER
Relationship
SMILE

Contents

Chapter	Page
Why Use a Communication Book	7
Suggestions	9-12
Sharing Information	13-319

Why use a communication book?

Why use a communication book?

□ Parental communication is a vital part of any co-parenting arrangement.

□ Conflict is a stumbling block to co-parenting, and direct communications can become strained.

□ Participation is voluntary. Both parents are aware that they are jointly sharing information for the benefit of their children because they want to.

□ This communication book provides a space for simple short child-focused communications.

□ It might help parents to become more child-focused in their communications.

□ It facilitates the sharing of small parts of childhood experiences.

□ A communication book might help to reduce anxiety or stress during handovers.

There are, of course, no guarantees.

Suggestions:

- A communication book is often used to assist positive co-parenting.

- There are no rules on how to complete a communication book.

- There are no sections in the main body of the communications book.

- Images have been incorporated to help parents keep child-focused.

That said parents might wish to consider the following:

- Parents should decide how they want to use a communication book.

- If parents need advice on how to complete a communication book, the advantages, and disadvantages of using this method of communication, they should seek advice from a professional advisor before they start using this method of communication.

- Decide on other methods of communication for:

-Time-sensitive;

-Urgent communications (regarding health, accidents, and hospital attendance, and short-notice changes, etc.); or

-Other sensitive or confidential information sharing.

This book is not suitable for urgent and confidential communications. Other methods of contact would be better. Parents should discuss and agree on the best way of sharing vital information.

- Keep communications short unless there is a specific reason for detail or length.

- Generally, entries are a few lines.

- Be polite, considerate, civil, and kind.

- Thank the other parent; it creates a more civil discourse.

- Keep communications as civil-exchanges, thus no accusations, complaints, or criticism.

- A communication book is not a complaints log.

- Consider how the other parent might receive or interpret an entry.

- No lectures on parenting skills.

- No attempts at one-upmanship.

- It's not a competition.

- Stick to the facts.

- Be accurate.

☐ Make requests, not demands.

☐ Choose your words carefully.

☐ Do not avoid or delay sharing information that would be in the child's best interests to share.

☐ Parents often worry about the reaction of the other parent if an incident occurs in their care. Take a child-focused approach – share information in a factually accurate and in a timely way; via a method of communication that is appropriate for the seriousness of the incident.

☐ Share information related to health immediately.

☐ Failure to or delay in sharing information regarding the school, extracurricular activities, party invitations, etc. is a source of general annoyance to parents. Take a child-focused approach; share information.

☐ Consider other safe methods of communication if you feel an amicable discussion is needed, such as mediation, family therapy, a parenting workshop, or other professional services.

☐ Consider drafting-out an entry first to ensure that it is child-focused.

☐ Date your entry. Sign as 'Mum' or 'Dad'.

☐ Discuss with the other parent the frequency

of entries, whether entries should be daily, an overview, or just related to significant areas of information sharing - e.g., homework.

 Be mindful that professionals might read the communications book.

 Remember that this book could be misplaced, lost, or stolen. Do not enter sensitive/ confidential information in a communication book. If you wish to share confidential information with the other parent use another method of communication, do not use this communication book.

From:

To:

Share their amazing news

- The children went to the park today and ran down the hill. They really loved it.

School friends

Sharing assembly

Native American Heritage Month

Fun Day

Clubs

Black History Month

Grandparents Day

School Lunch

Bring a picture of your family

Photos

School News

School Trips

Draw your family tree

Party invitations

School Fees

Games kit

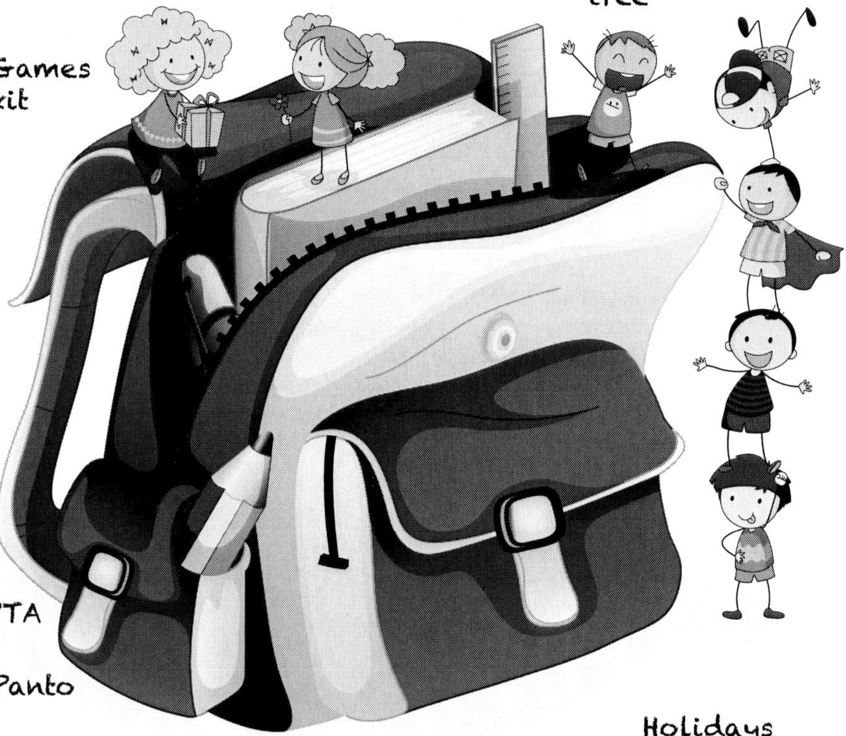

PTA

Panto

Holidays

Homework

Non School Uniform Day

WhatsApp groups

Open day

School events

Term time

School uniform

Concert

Sports day

Lock Down

Parents evening

World Book Day

Play

School Fête

Half Term

Reading Challenges

Exams

School Reports

Date Sharing Information

Signed

Date Sharing Information

Signed

Date Sharing Information

Signed

Date Sharing Information

Signed

Date Sharing Information

Signed

Date Sharing Information

Signed

Consider their timetable and when homework is due.

Share the parent homework signature book
Share their equipment, games kit and uniform etc.

It's their stuff no matter who purchased it
Take a child focused approach.

Date Sharing Information

Signed

Date Sharing Information

Signed

Date Sharing Information

Signed

Date Sharing Information

Signed

Date Sharing Information

Signed

Date Sharing Information

Signed

sad

frown

worry

emotions

Share

smile

laugh

cry

Date Sharing Information

Signed

Date Sharing Information

Signed

Date Sharing Information

Signed

Date Sharing Information

Signed

Date Sharing Information

Signed

Date Sharing Information

Signed

Share

Share

Date Sharing Information

Signed

Date Sharing Information

Signed

Date Sharing Information

Signed

Date Sharing Information

Signed

Date Sharing Information

Signed

Date Sharing Information

Signed

Share

Seeing a professional,
share the details

Share

Date Sharing Information

Signed

Date Sharing Information

Signed

Date Sharing Information

Signed

Date Sharing Information

Signed

Date Sharing Information

Signed

Date Sharing Information

Signed

Share details about accidents immediately

Share details about tests, treatment, and follow-ups immediately

Date Sharing Information

Signed

Date Sharing Information

Signed

Date Sharing Information

Signed

Date Sharing Information

Signed

Date Sharing Information

Signed

Date Sharing Information

Signed

Date Sharing Information

Signed

Date Sharing Information

Signed

Date Sharing Information

Signed

Date Sharing Information

Signed

Date Sharing Information

Signed

Date Sharing Information

Signed

Are the children seeing a professional?
Share the details.

Date Sharing Information

Signed

Date Sharing Information

Signed

Date Sharing Information

Signed

Date Sharing Information

Signed

Date Sharing Information

Signed

Date Sharing Information

Signed

Date Sharing Information

Signed

Date Sharing Information

Signed

Date Sharing Information

Signed

Date Sharing Information

Signed

Date Sharing Information

Signed

Date Sharing Information

Signed

Date Sharing Information

Signed

Date Sharing Information

Signed

Date Sharing Information

Signed

Date Sharing Information

Signed

Date Sharing Information

Signed

Date Sharing Information

Signed

Date Sharing Information

Signed

Date Sharing Information

Signed

Date Sharing Information

Signed

Date Sharing Information

Signed

Busy Being Awesome

Date Sharing Information

Signed

Date Sharing Information

Signed

Date Sharing Information

Signed

Date Sharing Information

Signed

Date Sharing Information

Signed

Date Sharing Information

Signed

Date Sharing Information

Signed

Date Sharing Information

Signed

Date Sharing Information

Signed

Date Sharing Information

Signed

Date Sharing Information

Signed

Date Sharing Information

Signed

Happy Birthday

Share how they spent their time

Date Sharing Information

Signed

Date Sharing Information

Signed

Date Sharing Information

Signed

Date Sharing Information

Signed

Date Sharing Information

Signed

Date Sharing Information

Signed

Date Sharing Information

Signed

Date Sharing Information

Signed

Date Sharing Information

Signed

Date Sharing Information

Signed

Date Sharing Information

Signed

Date Sharing Information

Signed

Date Sharing Information

Signed

Date Sharing Information

Signed

Date Sharing Information

Signed

Date Sharing Information

Signed

Best
Dad
Best
Son

Date Sharing Information

Signed

Date Sharing Information

Signed

Date Sharing Information

Signed

Date Sharing Information

Signed

Date Sharing Information

Signed

Date Sharing Information

Signed

Date Sharing Information

Signed

Date Sharing Information

Signed

Date Sharing Information

Signed

Date Sharing Information

Signed

Date Sharing Information

Signed

Date Sharing Information

Signed

Skills

Date Sharing Information

Signed

Date Sharing Information

Signed

Date Sharing Information

Signed

Date Sharing Information

Signed

Date Sharing Information

Signed

Date Sharing Information

Signed

Date Sharing Information

Signed

Date Sharing Information

Signed

Date Sharing Information

Signed

Date Sharing Information

Signed

Date Sharing Information

Signed

Date Sharing Information

Signed

Date Sharing Information

Signed

Date Sharing Information

Signed

Date Sharing Information

Signed

Date Sharing Information

Signed

Date Sharing Information

Signed

Date Sharing Information

Signed

Date Sharing Information

Signed

Date Sharing Information

Signed

Superhero

Date Sharing Information

Signed

Date Sharing Information

Signed

Date Sharing Information

Signed

Date Sharing Information

Signed

Date Sharing Information

Signed

Date Sharing Information

Signed

Date Sharing Information

Signed

Date Sharing Information

Signed

Date Sharing Information

Signed

Date Sharing Information

Signed

Date Sharing Information

Signed

Date Sharing Information

Signed

Date Sharing Information

Signed

Date Sharing Information

Signed

Date Sharing Information

Signed

Date Sharing Information

Signed

Date Sharing Information

Signed

Date Sharing Information

Signed

Date Sharing Information

Signed

Date Sharing Information

Signed

School Project
Share

Date Sharing Information

Signed

Date Sharing Information

Signed

Date Sharing Information

Signed

Date Sharing Information

Signed

Date Sharing Information

Signed

Date Sharing Information

Signed

Date Sharing Information

Signed

Date Sharing Information

Signed

Date Sharing Information

Signed

Date Sharing Information

Signed

He can stack all the coloured circles in order by himself

Date Sharing Information

Signed

Date Sharing Information

Signed

Date Sharing Information

Signed

Date Sharing Information

Signed

Date Sharing Information

Signed

Date Sharing Information

Signed

Date Sharing Information

Signed

Date Sharing Information

Signed

Date Sharing Information

Signed

Date Sharing Information

Signed

Date Sharing Information

Signed

Date Sharing Information

Signed

Date Sharing Information

Signed

Date Sharing Information

Signed

Date Sharing Information

Signed

Date Sharing Information

Signed

Date Sharing Information

Signed

Date Sharing Information

Signed

Date Sharing Information

Signed

Date Sharing Information

Signed

Date Sharing Information

Signed

Date Sharing Information

Signed

They practiced with their
hula hoops today

Date Sharing Information

Signed

Date Sharing Information

Signed

Date Sharing Information

Signed

Date Sharing Information

Signed

Date Sharing Information

Signed

Date Sharing Information

Signed

Date Sharing Information

Signed

Date Sharing Information

Signed

Date Sharing Information

Signed

Date Sharing Information

Signed

Date Sharing Information

Signed

Date Sharing Information

Signed

Date Sharing Information

Signed

Date Sharing Information

Signed

Date Sharing Information

Signed

Date Sharing Information

Signed

Date Sharing Information

Signed

Date Sharing Information

Signed

Date Sharing Information

Signed

Date Sharing Information

Signed

Date Sharing Information

Signed

Date Sharing Information

Signed

Date Sharing Information

Signed

Date Sharing Information

Signed

Date	Sharing Information

Signed

Date	Sharing Information

Signed

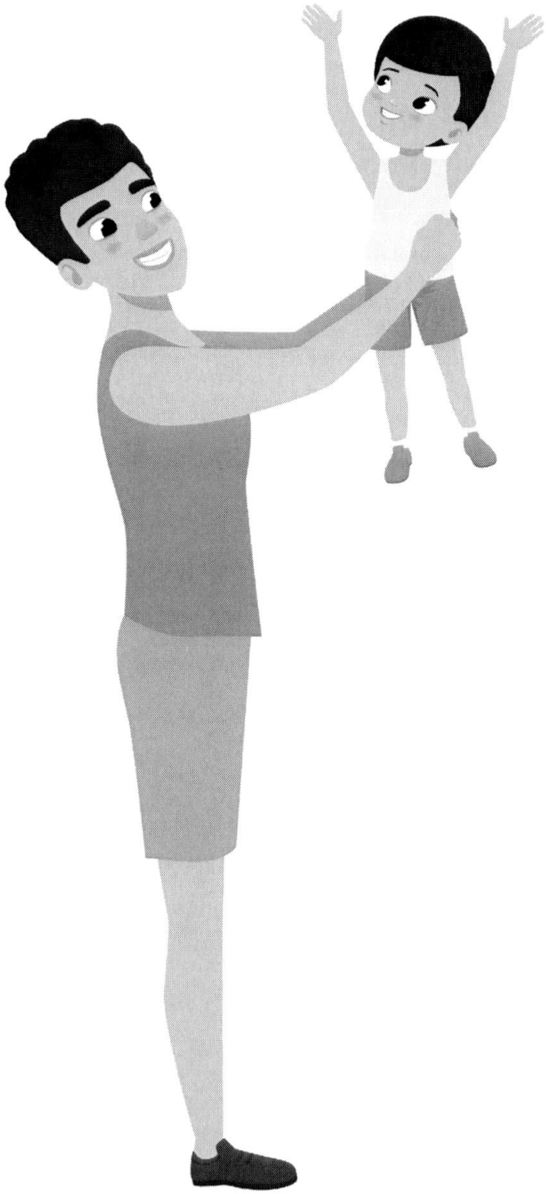

Date Sharing Information

Signed

Date Sharing Information

Signed

Date Sharing Information

Signed

Date Sharing Information

Signed

Date Sharing Information

Signed

Date Sharing Information

Signed

Date Sharing Information

Signed

Date Sharing Information

Signed

Date Sharing Information

Signed

Date Sharing Information

Signed

We played dolls today

Date Sharing Information

Signed

Date Sharing Information

Signed

Date Sharing Information

Signed

Date Sharing Information

Signed

Date Sharing Information

Signed

Date Sharing Information

Signed

Date Sharing Information

Signed

Date Sharing Information

Signed

Date Sharing Information

Signed

Date Sharing Information

Signed

Date Sharing Information

Signed

Date Sharing Information

Signed

Date Sharing Information

Signed

Date Sharing Information

Signed

Date Sharing Information

Signed

Date Sharing Information

Signed

SPORT

Date Sharing Information

Signed

Date Sharing Information

Signed

Date Sharing Information

Signed

Date Sharing Information

Signed

Date Sharing Information

Signed

Date Sharing Information

Signed

Date Sharing Information

Signed

Date Sharing Information

Signed

Date Sharing Information

Signed

Date Sharing Information

Signed

Date Sharing Information

Signed

Date Sharing Information

Signed

Date Sharing Information

Signed

Date Sharing Information

Signed

Date Sharing Information

Signed

Date Sharing Information

Signed

Date Sharing Information

Signed

Date Sharing Information

Signed

Date Sharing Information

Signed

Date Sharing Information

Signed

Date Sharing Information

Signed

Date Sharing Information

Signed

Date Sharing Information

Signed

Date Sharing Information

Signed

Date Sharing Information

Signed

Date Sharing Information

Signed

Date Sharing Information

Signed

Date Sharing Information

Signed

Date Sharing Information

Signed

Date Sharing Information

Signed

Date Sharing Information

Signed

Date Sharing Information

Signed

Date Sharing Information

Signed

Date Sharing Information

Signed

Accidents happen
Share the details immediately

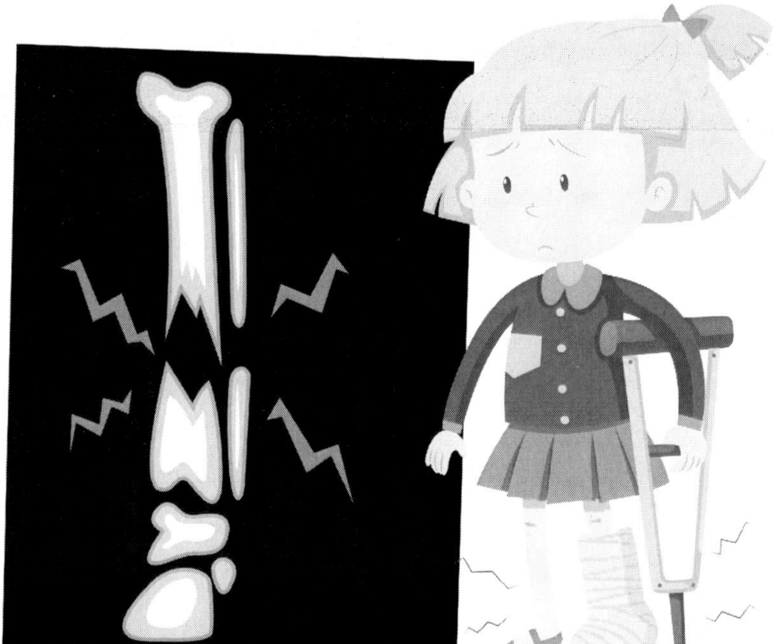

Date	Sharing Information

Signed

Date	Sharing Information

Signed

Date Sharing Information

Signed

Date Sharing Information

Signed

Date Sharing Information

Signed

Date Sharing Information

Signed

Coughing
Share

Date Sharing Information

Signed

Date Sharing Information

Signed

Date Sharing Information

Signed

Date Sharing Information

Signed

Date Sharing Information

Signed

Date Sharing Information

Signed

Head Lice
Share Information

Date Sharing Information

Signed

Date Sharing Information

Signed

Date Sharing Information

Signed

Date Sharing Information

Signed

Date Sharing Information

Signed

Date Sharing Information

Signed

Date Sharing Information

Signed

Date Sharing Information

Signed

Date Sharing Information

Signed

Date Sharing Information

Signed

Date Sharing Information

Signed

Date Sharing Information

Signed

Date Sharing Information

Signed

Date Sharing Information

Signed

Date Sharing Information

Signed

Date Sharing Information

Signed

Date Sharing Information

Signed

Date Sharing Information

Signed

Date Sharing Information

Signed

Date Sharing Information

Signed

Date Sharing Information

Signed

Date Sharing Information

Signed

Date Sharing Information

Signed

Date Sharing Information

Signed

Date Sharing Information

Signed

Date Sharing Information

Signed

Date Sharing Information

Signed

Date Sharing Information

Signed

Date Sharing Information

Signed

Date Sharing Information

Signed

Date Sharing Information

Signed

Date Sharing Information

Signed

Date Sharing Information

Signed

Date Sharing Information

Signed

Date Sharing Information

Signed

Date Sharing Information

Signed

Date Sharing Information

Signed

Date Sharing Information

Signed

Date Sharing Information

Signed

Date Sharing Information

Signed

Date Sharing Information

Signed

Date Sharing Information

Signed

Date Sharing Information

Signed

Date Sharing Information

Signed

Date Sharing Information

Signed

Date Sharing Information

Signed

Date Sharing Information

Signed

Date Sharing Information

Signed

Date Sharing Information

Signed

Date Sharing Information

Signed

Date Sharing Information

Signed

Date Sharing Information

Signed

Date Sharing Information

Signed

Date Sharing Information

Signed

Date Sharing Information

Signed

Date Sharing Information

Signed

Date Sharing Information

Signed

Date Sharing Information

Signed

Date Sharing Information

Signed

Date Sharing Information

Signed

Date	Sharing Information
Signed	

Date	Sharing Information
Signed	

Date Sharing Information

Signed

Date Sharing Information

Signed

Date Sharing Information

Signed

Date Sharing Information

Signed

Date Sharing Information

Signed

Date Sharing Information

Signed

Date Sharing Information

Signed

Date Sharing Information

Signed

Date Sharing Information

Signed

Date Sharing Information

Signed

Take a child focused approach to each other's birthday.

Would the child like to give their parent a birthday card or present?

Date Sharing Information

Signed

Date Sharing Information

Signed

Date Sharing Information

Signed

Date Sharing Information

Signed

Date Sharing Information

Signed

Date Sharing Information

Signed

Date Sharing Information

Signed

Date Sharing Information

Signed

Date Sharing Information

Signed

Date Sharing Information

Signed

Date Sharing Information

Signed

Date Sharing Information

Signed

Date Sharing Information

Signed

Date Sharing Information

Signed

Date Sharing Information

Signed

Date Sharing Information

Signed

Date Sharing Information

Signed

Date Sharing Information

Signed

Date Sharing Information

Signed

Date Sharing Information

Signed

Date Sharing Information

Signed

Date Sharing Information

Signed

Date Sharing Information

Signed

Date Sharing Information

Signed

Date Sharing Information

Signed

Date Sharing Information

Signed

Date Sharing Information

Signed

Date Sharing Information

Signed

Date Sharing Information

Signed

Date Sharing Information

Signed

Date Sharing Information

Signed

Date Sharing Information

Signed

Date Sharing Information

Signed

Date Sharing Information

Signed

Date Sharing Information

Signed

Date Sharing Information

Signed

Date Sharing Information

Signed

Date Sharing Information

Signed

Joy
Share

Date Sharing Information

Signed

Date Sharing Information

Signed

Date Sharing Information

Signed

Date Sharing Information

Signed

Date Sharing Information

Signed

Date Sharing Information

Signed

Date Sharing Information

Signed

Date Sharing Information

Signed

Date Sharing Information

Signed

Date Sharing Information

Signed

Date Sharing Information

Signed

Date Sharing Information

Signed

Date Sharing Information

Signed

Date Sharing Information

Signed

Date Sharing Information

Signed

Date Sharing Information

Signed

Date Sharing Information

Signed

Date Sharing Information

Signed

Date Sharing Information

Signed

Date Sharing Information

Signed

Holidays - Share Their News

Date Sharing Information

Signed

Date Sharing Information

Signed

Date Sharing Information

Signed

Date Sharing Information

Signed

Date Sharing Information

Signed

Date Sharing Information

Signed

Date Sharing Information

Signed

Date Sharing Information

Signed

Date Sharing Information

Signed

Date Sharing Information

Signed

Date Sharing Information

Signed

Date Sharing Information

Signed

Date Sharing Information

Signed

Date Sharing Information

Signed

In an emergency share information immediately

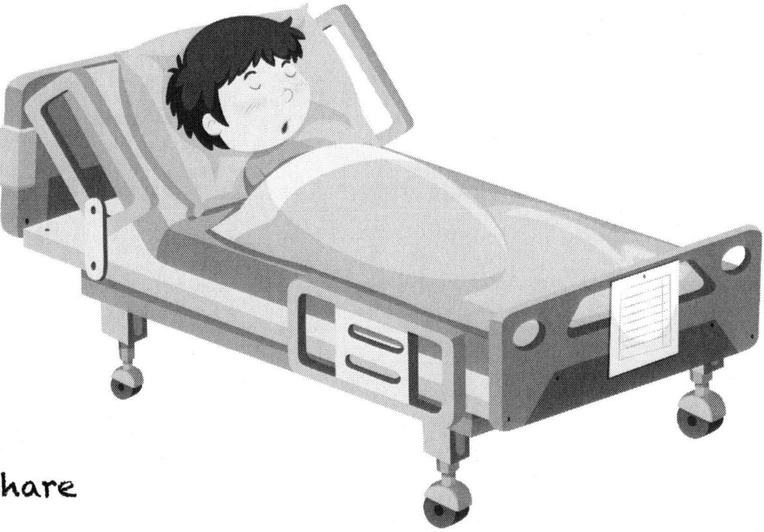

Share

Share

Date Sharing Information

Signed

Date Sharing Information

Signed

Date Sharing Information

Signed

Date Sharing Information

Signed

Date Sharing Information

Signed

Date Sharing Information

Signed

Date Sharing Information

Signed

Date Sharing Information

Signed

Date Sharing Information

Signed

Date Sharing Information

Signed

Unwell
Share

Date Sharing Information

Signed

Date Sharing Information

Signed

Date Sharing Information

Signed

Date Sharing Information

Signed

Date Sharing Information

Signed

Date Sharing Information

Signed

Date Sharing Information

Signed

Date Sharing Information

Signed

Date Sharing Information

Signed

Date Sharing Information

Signed

Date Sharing Information

Signed

Date Sharing Information

Signed

Date Sharing Information

Signed

Date Sharing Information

Signed

Chicken Pox
Share

Date Sharing Information

Signed

Date Sharing Information

Signed

Date Sharing Information

Signed

Date Sharing Information

Signed

Date Sharing Information

Signed

Date Sharing Information

Signed

Share child focused information so that both parents can provide support

Date Sharing Information

Signed

Date Sharing Information

Signed

Date Sharing Information

Signed

Date Sharing Information

Signed

Date Sharing Information

Signed

Date Sharing Information

Signed

Date Sharing Information

Signed

Date Sharing Information

Signed

Date Sharing Information

Signed

Date Sharing Information

Signed

Share child focused information so that both parents can provide support

Date Sharing Information

Signed

Date Sharing Information

Signed

Date Sharing Information

Signed

Date Sharing Information

Signed

Date Sharing Information

Signed

Date Sharing Information

Signed

Date Sharing Information

Signed

Date Sharing Information

Signed

Date Sharing Information

Signed

Date Sharing Information

Signed

Date Sharing Information

Signed

Date Sharing Information

Signed

Date Sharing Information

Signed

Date Sharing Information

Signed

Date Sharing Information

Signed

Date Sharing Information

Signed

Date Sharing Information

Signed

Date Sharing Information

Signed

Date Sharing Information

Signed

Date Sharing Information

Signed

Date Sharing Information

Signed

Date Sharing Information

Signed

Date Sharing Information

Signed

Date Sharing Information

Signed

Date Sharing Information

Signed

Date Sharing Information

Signed

Date Sharing Information

Signed

Date Sharing Information

Signed

Date Sharing Information

Signed

Date Sharing Information

Signed

Date Sharing Information

Signed

Date Sharing Information

Signed

Date Sharing Information

Signed

Date Sharing Information

Signed

Grandfa
Grandma
FAMILY
lovely
FRIENDS
MOMMY
uncle
PARENTS
Sweet
I ♥ my family
AUNT
Grand parents
MOTHER
DADDY
son
SISTER
Home
FATHER
BROTHER
Relationship
SMILE

Made in United States
North Haven, CT
10 November 2026

22095604R00176